Russell Grant's
Art of Astrology

BLINK
bringing you closer

Published by Blink Publishing
3.25, The Plaza,
535 Kings Road,
Chelsea Harbour,
London, SW10 0SZ

www.blinkpublishing.co.uk

facebook.com/blinkpublishing
twitter.com/blinkpublishing

ISBN 978-1-910536-65-0

A CIP catalogue of this book is available from the British Library.

Printed in the UK

3 5 7 9 10 8 6 4 2

Papers used by Blink Publishing are natural, recyclable products made from wood grown in sustainable forests. The manufacturing processes conform to the environmental regulations of the country of origin.

Blink Publishing is an imprint of the Bonnier Publishing Group
www.bonnierpublishing.co.uk

Contents

Introduction

In the last 50 years or so that I have been involved in teaching and studying astrology, people seem to have become more and more confused about what it actually is.

The problem lies, in part, with the incredible growth of the internet and social media, and the mixed messages they have spread.

Today, people have access to so many sources, from print articles to websites and apps dedicated to 'predicting the future' via 'star signs', that there has been a widespread misconception that this is astrology's sole purpose. It might surprise some of you to know that astrology does not predict.

I believe that astrology is a key, a tool, a passport that unlocks the door to a detailed understanding of who we are, what forces are at work within us and how we can capitalise on them. Essentially, astrology tells us what we as individuals can do and what we are capable of. It reveals our potential. Once we understand this, we are free to fulfil that potential to the absolute maximum.

In my *Art of Astrology* we are only dealing with the Sun signs. Just as the Sun dominates the solar system, so it casts a giant shadow over astrology and the astrological planets. The Sun sign (often called a star sign or zodiac sign) is actually the sign of the zodiac where the Sun was placed when you were born. Along with the Ascending or Rising sign (based on your time and place of birth) and the Moon sign, the Sun sign is all-powerful. It is our creative heart and soul, our true self.

Whilst this book only looks at the Sun sign, if you want to know where the rest of your planets are you might get a clue once you've read through the interpretation of the Sun signs. As you read all the signs, others might chime with you, which is perfectly possible, as one of the other planets could be in that sign in your chart.

To get more information for free, go to my website, www.russellgrant.com, where with your date, time and place of birth you can get your own natal chart that lists your planets from the Sun right through to Pluto (if you're on the cusp, your natal chart will tell you which sign the Sun is actually in).

Now, whether you're an astrology amateur or a cosmic connoisseur, I invite you to enjoy these illustrations, colour them in however you would like and discover what the colours you've chosen say about you.

The Cusp

You will notice that the dates here might not match those you are familiar with. This is because, contrary to popular belief, the signs do not change at midnight on a given day; it is not that cut-and-dry. If you take into account the various other factors at play, the Sun might enter Aries a day earlier or later each year. They can also change morning, noon or night. So the dates in periodicals and websites are, in general, only ever approximate. Now you see why your birth time is so crucial.

How to use

My fascination with colour began when I was very young, raised in the leafy village of Harefield in Middlesex. Kids of my age usually went out to play sports or games (no Xbox or the like then!) but I stayed in with a stack of colouring books and crayons. I even remember making a model theatre, designing scenery and costumes at the age of seven. A regular mark of 'A+' in my junior school results for Art made me wonder if it should be my vocation.

I also wanted to be a Geography or History teacher, which were great loves of mine, and, in time, my passion led me to write two history books that made the bestseller lists: *The Real Counties of Britain* and *A History of the City of Gloucester*. My mother and father were both in the movie industry, my uncle (Mum's brother) went on to win an Oscar for *The Deer Hunter*. Mum wanted me to go to drama school nearby, so I did, to an outreach of LAMDA. I suddenly found myself acting and singing, but an innate love of colour and art never left me, and has stayed with me ever since.

In my early teens I discovered the local Spiritualist group and soon my own psychic world was filled with colour. Psychic development uses the chakra, those parts of the body resonating and vibrating to colours of the rainbow, to work on. I presented a documentary on feng shui for ITV and it really gave me a chance to utilise my love of colour, and since then that is what I have been doing more than ever: colour design for homes and offices using my newly acquired (well, a decade of) knowledge in this ancient Chinese discipline.

The best way to use this colouring book is not to think about how things are in the natural order, like green grass or white snow. Instead, let your imagination and intuition fly free. If you'll allow me to guide you, here is what I suggest…

1. Find a quiet or favourite place – where you feel at one with the world, calm and comfortable inside.

2. Candles are great for inspiration: perhaps in your favourite colour, with a fragrance that wafts around and takes you to wonderful memories or a good time in your life where you felt joy or happiness. A water feature can also work well, as the sounds of tinkling water can work wonders for your intuition.

3. Music! Some find that silence is golden, others like to listen to their favourite piece serenading them. It can be classical or pop but blast it around the room when you are waiting for the muse to strike. Do not use through headphones, it will oversaturate the sound and cut you off from the colour-focus you need to inspire.

4. Then, if you've treated yourself to one of those sumptuous boxes of many-coloured pencils or squidgy paints in tubes that marry up to the 16 prime colours I have used in the book (check you have them), familiarise yourself with each.

5. This is the important bit – look at the page or design you want to colour and then gaze at your crayons, pencils or paint and go with the first one you are drawn to. Remember: you don't need to follow the rules; the golden rule is to please yourself and use the colour that attracts you and feels 'right'.

6. Start playing with the colours. Once you have finished your artwork, you might find one colour dominates all others; make a note of the colours that stand out and also those colours that are missing!

7. Once you've listed the colours that dominate, read its interpretation in my rainbow guide. Ask yourself: is this something I am missing in my personality or life? You might find it strikes a chord, as the colour sparks off something inside you, perhaps filling-in a missing spiritual, psychological or personality link.

8. Look at the missing colours in your drawing. Read the interpretation and ask: why did it not appeal to you? Is it because you have too much of its traits in your persona already or, possibly, not enough?

9. Colours you are drawn to will change regularly, maybe even daily. Like your aura (emotional, mental and spiritual radiation forming an energy field around the body, like a halo or aureola), one day it can be a beautiful blue (giving out or needing to receive healing) and the next yellow (need for learning and studying, giving or receiving knowledge).

10. Soak up the colours around you. Look at the art, décor or figurines in the room you are in, and figure out how it would be with different colours, shades and hues. The four walls, would they be better in something sparkling and vibrant, or cool and soothing, or in dual shades? Experiment with colours, for they are there to be enjoyed and played with.

Colour can bring great pleasure, and I now would like to wish you the joy and contentment that I have had while living with it on this planet.

Thank you for reading this.

Russell Grant

Snowdonia, North Wales/Gogledd Cymru – Autumn Equinox, 2015.

Aries

Approx. 21ˢᵗ March – 20ᵗʰ April

Aries is the first sign of the zodiac. The astrological New Year does not begin on 1ˢᵗ January but at the time of the vernal equinox or the first day of Spring (Autumn in the southern hemisphere). This can be anytime from 20ᵗʰ to 22ⁿᵈ of March, dependent on the year.

I've depicted the myth of macho-man Jason as the archetypal Aries, and his pursuit and capture of the Golden Fleece gives a double-whammy of Arian qualities. Jason's vitality and stamina makes him a hero and, after all, it is Aries the Ram he is determined to win!

Aries is the sign summed up by the personal ego. This is the assertion of the individual spirit that drives them to break from the crowd or collective to make their own name. Largely competitive, this is the sign that wants to win and is not inclined to see victory as anything other than a gold medal or first place.

The Aries ram takes the initiative and puts themselves forward to be a leader, but then there are also ewes or lambs that tend to follow the flock and prefer to play follow-my-leader. Sorting out the rams from the lambs boils down to the position of the ruler Mars in the natal chart, for this is the planetary force driving this fire sign.

As the first sign of the zodiac, Aries is a baby. No matter how old they are, there is a juvenile immaturity or charm which makes demands on people around them. People can pacify them but if Aries continues to yell it will try the patience of all the other signs, which leads to a damaging relationship where egos clash and everything falls apart.

The mature Aries is single-minded, inventive and totally committed to reaching their goal. When the going gets tough, the tough get going. That's Aries for you – Jason all the way.

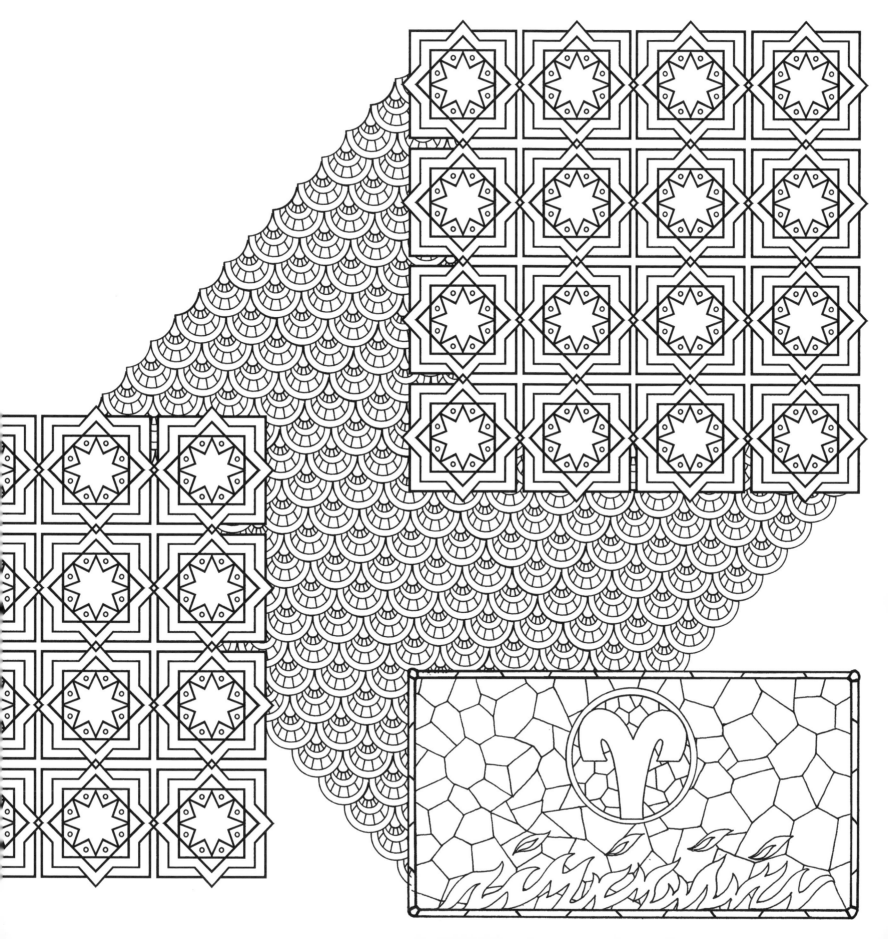

Taurus

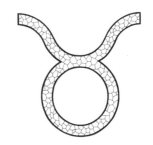

Approx. 21st April – 20th May

Once Aries has conquered, then Taurus lays down foundations. The Venus connection here is very different to the Venus that rules Libra. This Venus is sensual, earthy and passionate. Taurus is precisely the same; form, body and desire emanate from this second sign of the zodiac.

There are many bovine myths, but one of the most famous is The Minotaur eventually killed by Theseus with clever cunning and connivance. Equally legendary is the myth of the nymph Europa. When Zeus (or Jupiter) admired her beauty and wished to ravish her, he turned himself into a bull so that he may adore her. There is also Ishtar, the Venus of Babylonia, who sent a bull into battle at Gilgamesh to fight for her.

Taureans have a desire to possess and acquire. For them, 'the tangible' is the only thing worth having. This earth sign once represented the beginning of the zodiac. In Egypt, it was when Taurus was high in the heavens that cattle and oxen ploughed the fields. Taurus rules abundance and fertility, whether it is food or sex.

The notoriety of Taureans' stubbornness and obstinacy are keywords when summing up the more negative traits of The Bull. But what do you expect? This animal is not going to be shifted once it has been set on its furrowed course, so human Bulls born under this earthiest of earth signs aren't going to be budged once their mind is made up.

But if you can tame the negative qualities then more positive energies come powering through in the form of fidelity, loyalty and pragmatism. 'Fecund' is a delicious word for this voluptuous Venusian.

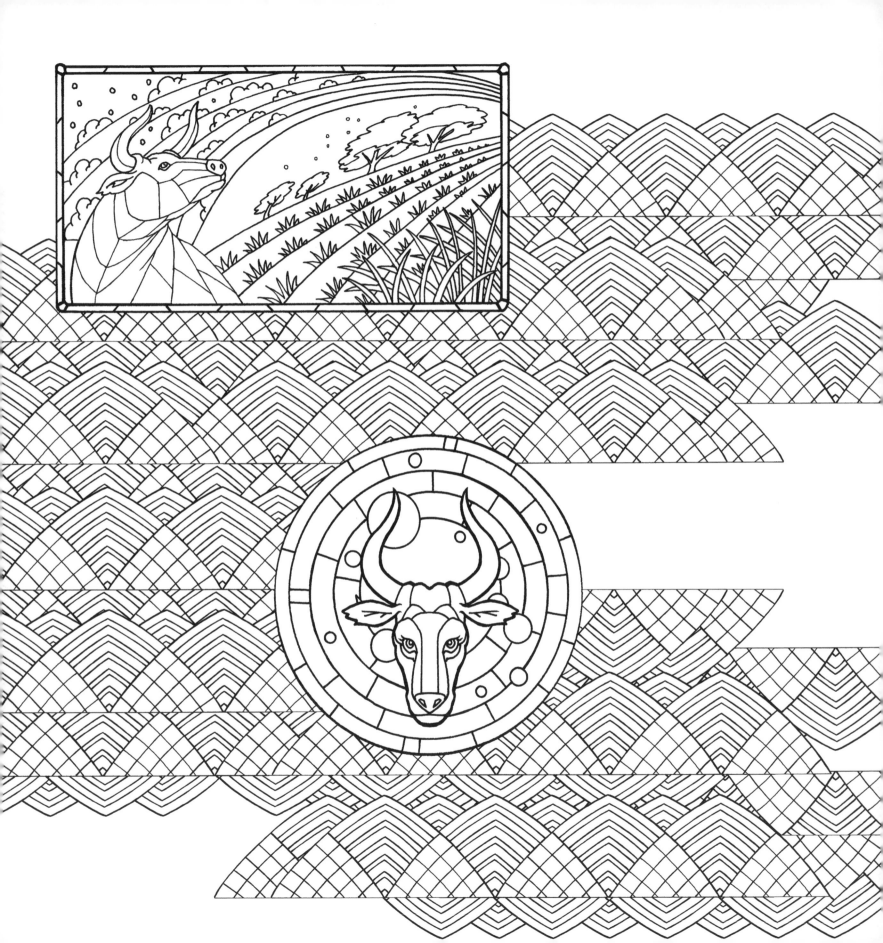

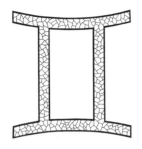

Gemini

Approx. 21st May – 21st June

Gemini is much more complex than you would at first suppose. It's usually Scorpio that wears the accolade of being the perennial riddle wrapped in an enigma at the centre of a mystery, but this air sign has many psychological contortions going on.

This is due to the sign's Mercury ruler; this planet always has one side always facing the sun and is bright and light, which means that the other side is in perpetual darkness, intense and brooding. That's it in a nutshell.

The twins Castor and Pollux, one of whom was immortal, the other not, mirror this difference. The myth tells that when Castor, the mortal brother, died his human soul went to the underworld, so his brother offered to share his immortality at the cost of having to spend half his days away from heaven, in the underworld. Today, the brightest stars in the constellation of Gemini are called Castor and Pollux.

The sunny side of Gemini is ingenious, brilliant and the life-and-soul of the party with witty repartee; the sparkling raconteur. The dark side is moody, volatile, emotionally immature and unable to connect with people on a consistently serious level.

Like Peter Pan, this sign rarely grows up; forever young. They are the most incredible communicators with a brain that surpasses many of their peers. Their fragility lies in connecting the mind with the body with the spirit. Their dazzle lies in intellectual agility, which gives them an eternally inquiring mind.

Cancer

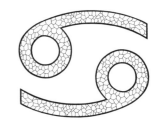

Approx. 22nd June – 23rd July

The Moon has been at the centre of romance, prose and poetry from the beginning of time. This encompasses the philosophy of the soft-centred sign of Cancer and the cosmic connection between it and the Moon since time immemorial.

Those within Cancer are nostalgic and sentimental but need to learn not to live in the past or they will find it hard to leave behind the bad and move on to the better times that await them.

The ancient Egyptians began their year during July and, for them, the powerful talisman of the Scarab beetle symbolised the point at which the soul or spirit entered the human body. Even now, it is said the Scarab has powerful protective energies when worn.

Cancer is the mother of all signs. 'Protection' is a word that sums up the maternal instincts of this lunar baby. The carapace gives secu-

rity against the wiles of a wicked world, for within this water sign is a soft core. Whether this be a beetle or a shelled crab hiding away from confrontation, they favour protection.

Cancer can be damaged if their early years are without the love of a family to nurture them. A secure home life in their early years will make for a well-adjusted and emotionally well-balanced soul.

An unhappy Crab is moody, sad and brittle. A happy one can resist hurt and embrace those they love and care for with stability and emotional roots that last forever.

Leo

Approx. 24th July – 23rd August

If you ever try to stare at the Sun (and please don't) it would blind you. Leo's association with the centre of our solar system makes for a personality that shines brightly with radiant splendour. But gazing directly at a Leo in action can turn into a love-hate relationship. There is only one sun in the sky and a Leo, male or female, thinks the same. Be warned of their dazzling ego, as it can be pure Hollywood (with all the razzle-dazzle, showbiz and attention-seeking) and as a result you'll love 'em or hate 'em.

There are two prominent myths to suit this fire sign; the Nemean Lion (the first of Hercules's labours: he had to kill the cat) and the Sphinx: half-lion, half-goddess. The former suits better because it is less enigmatic and mysterious. However, there are Leos who shun the limelight and prefer to play a role behind the camera, rather than the star.

The glory of Leo comes through their supreme creativity and artistry; Apollo and Orpheus give a classical clue as to their fabulous potential. Apollo is the God of music and drama and Orpheus the representation of Apollo on earth – the God taught Orpheus how to play the lyre. Leo is the sign of love and music. Shakespeare's line 'If music be the food of love, play on' could have been written with Leo in mind.

Leo is the sign of the heart's desire. But the love and joy in their hearts is sometimes cursed by dominance and control, so the Lion must beware of only wanting to do things to get their own way.

Virgo

Approx. 24th August – 23rd September

Virgo is another dual sign. Like Gemini, it has dual qualities. However, the rulership of Mercury means that Virgo takes on a different tone, as an earth rather than air sign.

The intellectual might of Mercury is diffused into the need for a tidy, analytical, organised mind. An ordered approach topped with common-sense can lead to accusations of being unemotional. Of course, like other sun signs, no Virgo is the same and the position of the Moon in the natal chart in relation to the planets within will colour the feelings in different hues.

The most relevant stories within the classics are those of Ceres/Demeter (Goddess of the harvest), Hygeia and Athene/Minerva. The other significant tale is that of Demeter and Persephone, as the Goddess pines the loss of her daughter when for six months of every year Persephone descends back to Hades. The power of sacrifice is evident in Virgo.

Virgos are always available: they want to help, to give and to support. Virginal modesty without a thought for themselves is a key characteristic.

Should their Mercurial mind get muddled or confused, their personality and approach is polarised. They are untidy (with an uncanny knack of still knowing where everything is), as well as pedantic and interfering.

A positive Virgo is good to have around: they are instinctively life's helpers and a bulwark against life's users.

Libra

Approx. 24th September – 23rd October

Welcome to the fluffy, pink, candy-floss world of Venus! Libra is love. Libra loves to love. Libra falls in love with love. This is the Venus of Botticelli, as, in exaltation of the goddess of love, she rises from the surging waves in a pearly shell: the essence of beauty.

Librans love beautiful people and revile anything ugly or physically grotesque. The power of initial attraction can lead this air sign into difficult relationships. They need balance (which inspires their zodiac symbol) and to know that beauty is often more from within than without. But they find it hard to be with anyone intimately unless they are gorgeous.

Usually they fail to dump so wait for the other person to leave, as they don't (a) like to make the decision, and (b) to hurt anyone. This means they will stay in a bad relationship even though they know it isn't ever going to work out. They hate being on their own.

Libra is the sign for relationships.

A balance is the key to their happiness. Too much of one thing and not enough of the other can lead to disappointment and loneliness. In any partnership it should be half and half to work. The tale of Eros and Psyche sums this up perfectly: it is the story of love in search of a soul and a soul in search of love.

50

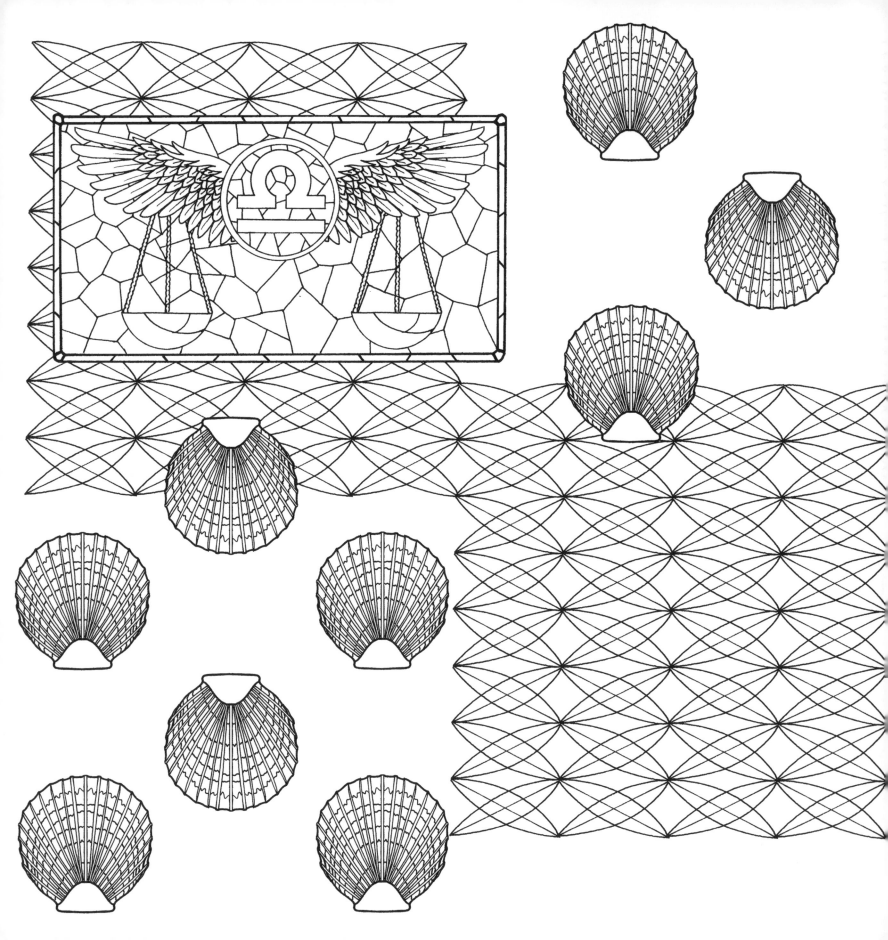

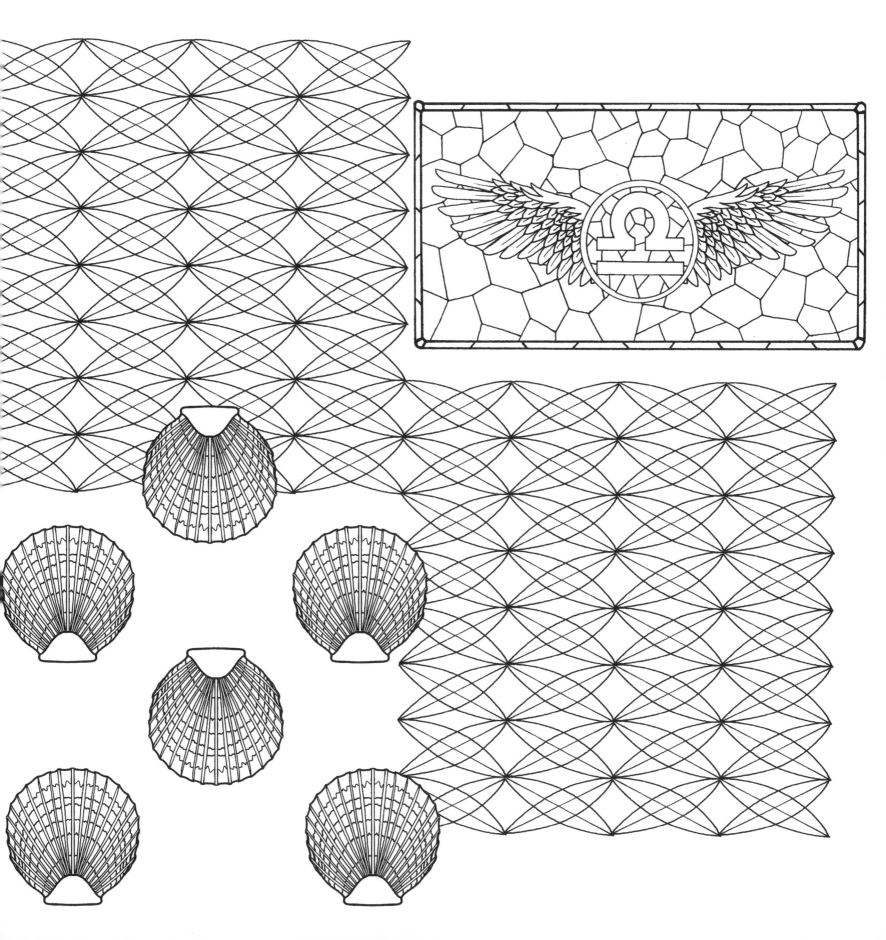

Scorpio

Approx. 24th October – 22nd November

Don't believe the press Scorpio gets as a sign. No it's not all doom and gloom, although there are many Scorpios who might revel in being the mafia of the zodiac (as in, they are secretive, controlling and vengeful).

Of course, being ruled by two of the most potent planetary powers, Mars and Pluto, adds to the myth of destruction. But with destruction comes renewal and the Phoenix illustrates this life/death sign perfectly; rising from the ashes and soaring to new heights in pursuit of rebirth and transformation.

The analogy of the iceberg is a good pointer to the personality of water sign Scorpio, as two-thirds of it is hidden from view. The mystery of Scorpio comes from wondering what is going on underneath. Still waters run deep. What you see isn't necessarily what you get. In fact, far from it, as obsession can often take over from sensible actions, as they can become fixated with anything or anyone.

Scorpio is an intense conundrum; they have a need for deep, psychological sexual experiences with an over-riding belief that fate has the final control over our lives and living. Vengeful, complicated and manipulative, you shouldn't play games with this potentially maleficent sign, as revenge will come swiftly!

No easy type to understand but if they want you in their world then they offer loyalty and passion, standing by you come what may. They will wage war on your enemies and be the army you need against wrongs and injustice.

Betray them and you will have an eternal enemy; adore them and you will have a friend for life.

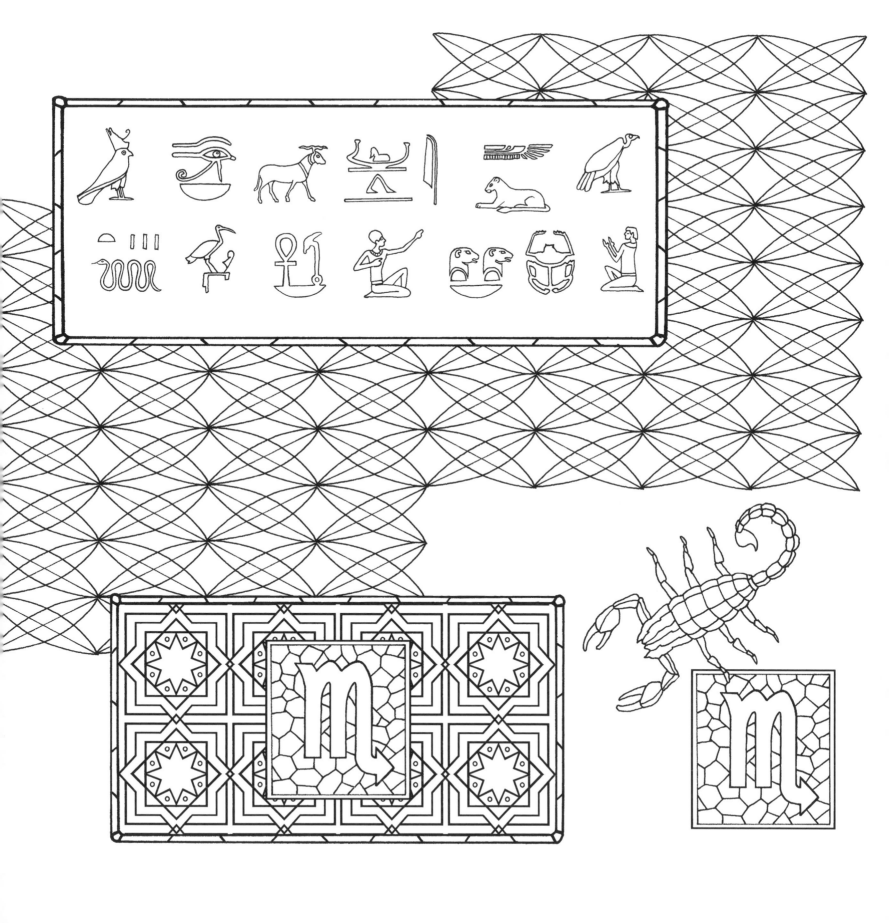

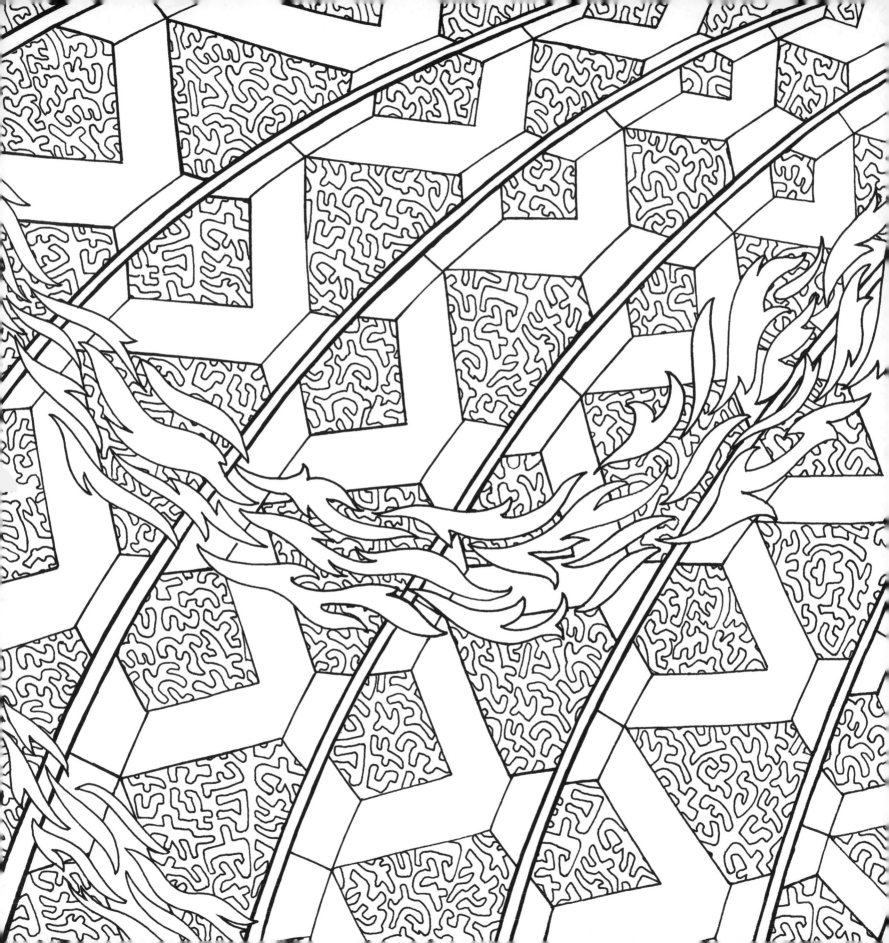

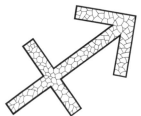

Sagittarius

Approx. 23rd November – 21st December

Sagittarius is a fire sign ruled by the king, the emperor of the heavens Jupiter. Timid and pessimistic people cut no ice with this sign of joy. Live for today!

But hold your horses! Not all Sagittarians are blithe and sanguine, some ARE doubtful and depressive, and that's because the rest of their chart could be heavy with challenging aspects from other planets.

This sign is the perfect pick-me-up and tonic. Have a Sagittarian handy if you're feeling blue, for they will soon lift you into a purple patch with their vitality-red spirit.

There is no doubt that Chiron the Centaur is their mythological symbol. The wounded soul, injured in his thigh and rendered immobile. There lies the biggest fear of the Sagittarian: the loss of freedom or the chance to travel and roam-free is anathema. The wild rover, buccaneer and adventurer, they are the great traveller. If this Jupiterian child is disabled physically then their mind takes over, as Chiron communicated his knowledge ranging from astrology to medicine, music to mathematics to anyone who inquired.

Prone to exaggeration and excess, take some things with a pinch of salt, as they will go over the top at times.

Capricorn

Approx. 22nd December – 20th January

Stepping up to the plate is something this ambitious sign will do time and time again. Unfazed and unmoved by challenge, Capricorn has tamed itself to focus on achieving whatever mountain they have chosen to climb.

Ruled by ringed Saturn, they can be self-critical and their own worst enemy through being self-limiting and can be restrictive with self-made rules and regulations that usually stem from their upbringing and a desperate need for approval from those around them. Suspicious and cautious, Saturnians find it hard to trust. From parents to teachers to bosses, they despise authority and yet can be most authoritarian.

The deity Pan is the mythic creature linked to Capricorn. This sign's sexual appetite and prowess is as driven as Scorpio's but with less passion and more earthly, primeval desires. The image of Pan has often been used to depict the devil and the goat's love of nature, as well as the things most raw and basic. This promises a person who can sometimes come across as vulgar and dissolute.

I call them 'the giddy goat'. They are characterised by laughter and a wry, dry sense of humour, which can be a gift to the stand-up comic, as they carry an astute sense of timing through their everyday life. Punctuality and tempus fugit is on their coat of arms. Slow but sure, Capricorn is the tortoise leaving behind the hare, those more impetuous signs.

Capricorn has a sense of destiny translated in their pursuit of success and prestige, recognition and achievement, for they know that if they have this then material wealth is sure to follow.

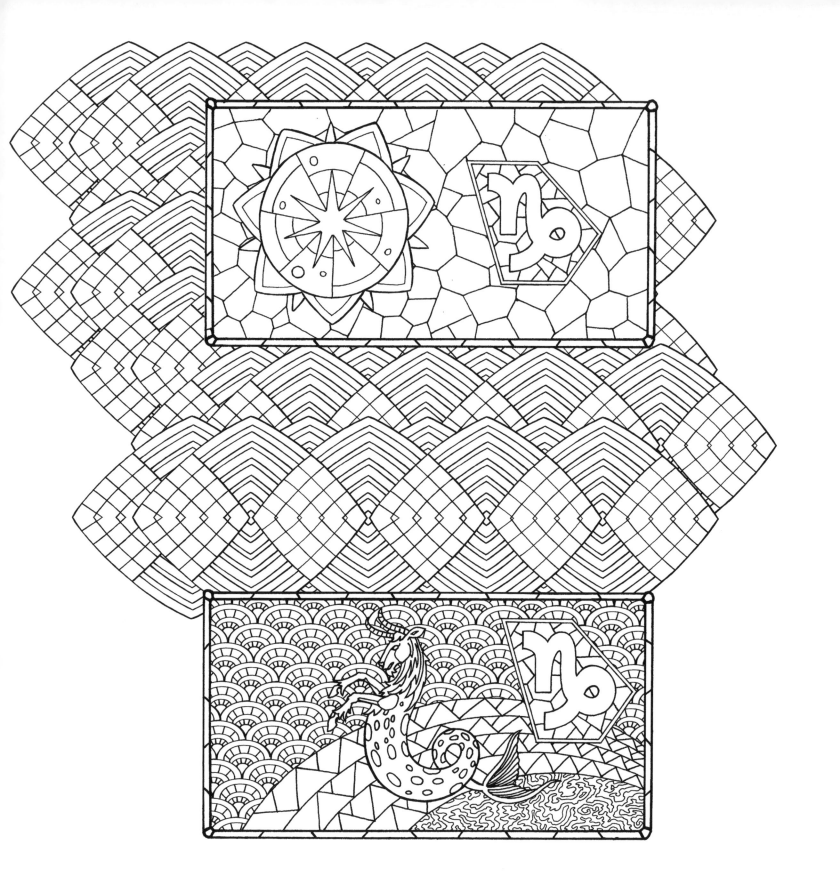

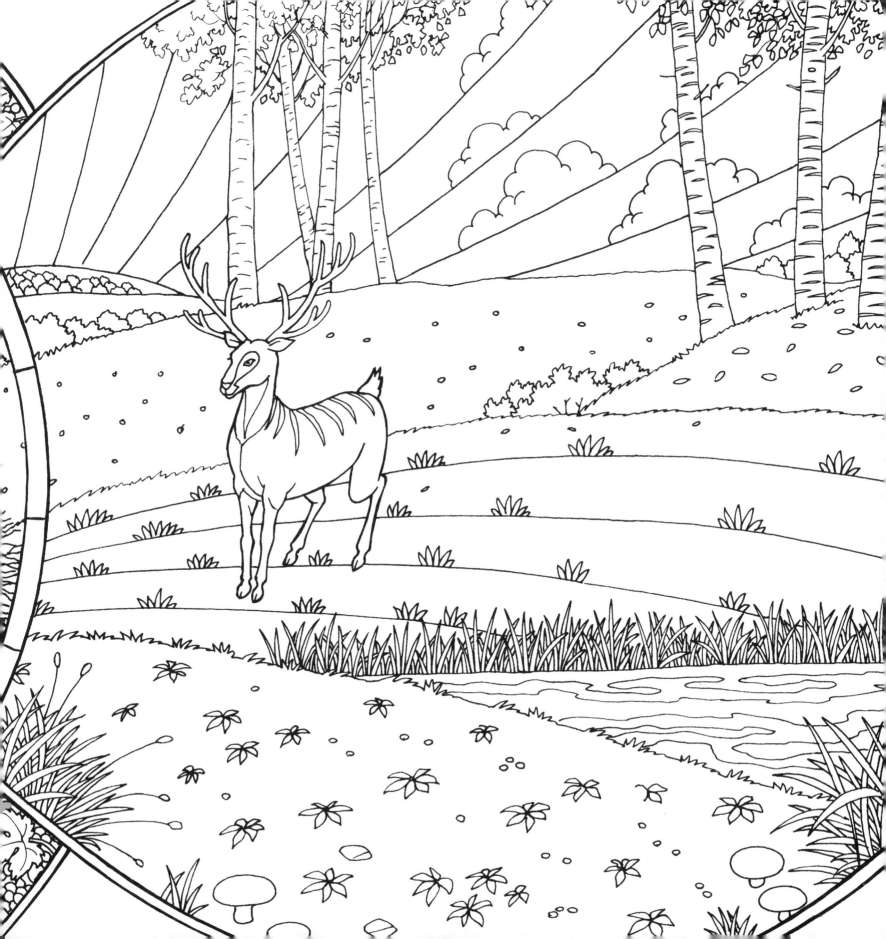

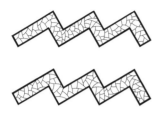

Aquarius

Approx. 21st January – 19th February

There is something strange about this sign. It is the sign of the future but those within it often resist moving on, instead cling to the past. Through the rulership of Uranus, they are eccentric and unpredictable charismatic, magnetic and electrifying. And yet, their traditional ruler Saturn wags his finger at the co-ruler, for the Aquarian can also hate waste and despise rejection, as well as fearing the future. Ironically, they are the sign of looking to the future but are often too scared to then go for it, fearing the unknown.

Instead of trying to fully understand this air (not water) sign, concentrate on its humanitarian side. The legend of Prometheus befits Aquarius. Look at the first paragraph again, for this sign can be tormented by a lack of intellectual freedom and it is through their human foibles they are kept earthbound and suffer as a result. They want to fly sky-high.

Unique and avant-garde, this rainbow sign is attracted to the unusual and outrageous, and yet they like the norm and want to conform. Yet again, another paradox, a dichotomy, more tension that exists within the confines of a Saturn world when the Uranian utopia is so near yet so far.

How do you solve a problem like Aquarius? The answer is: you probably never will and, the chances are, nor will the Aquarian. Their contradictory, bloody-mindedness coupled with cutting off their nose to spite their face and the desperate need to look for an escape if they feel imprisoned, especially emotionally, gives rise to a sign that will make the best of friends but can be difficult to live with or understand.

Pisces

Approx. 20th February – 20th March

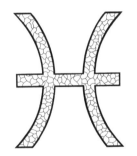

Pisces is a fish in all aspects. Some fishes go with the flow whilst others swim against the tide. Ruled by water, Pisces is one of the most emotional signs of the zodiac.

This sign is ruled by both Jupiter, the epitome of mythological royalty, and Neptune, the deity of the sea, but these two giants of Olympus didn't get on. Jupiter is all-powerful, flinging around thunderbolts every time he is challenged, and Neptune whips up a storm when confronted. This can be a timid, shy sign but also one that has the allure of enchantment and can use seduction to get their own way.

Caring, kind, sentimental, compassionate – that's Pisces. Addictive, in-denial, escapist, self-deceptive – that's the other side. So how do you get a handle on this sign of mystery – one I have always seen as the area of secrets and sorrows in the solar horoscope?

Think of the fish again, either swimming with or against the flow: they will cosset you with tender loving care or be an emotional wreck. Pisces can be a saint or a martyr, the sufferer or the victim.

With such sublime and well-developed senses, the Piscean intuition is clairvoyant or even psychic. However, the myth of Cassandra should be heeded. She was given the gift of prophecy but an angry Apollo made sure that nobody listened to her warnings. It is important for this fish to not live in a world of their own. They can use pretence and make-believe to brush over the harshness of the reality of modern life.

To go back to the idea of fish: one approach is seeking spiritual enlightenment (and Pisces can really benefit from contemplation, meditation and the gentle arts), whilst the other shows an intent towards material matters and gaining advancement through the mundane.

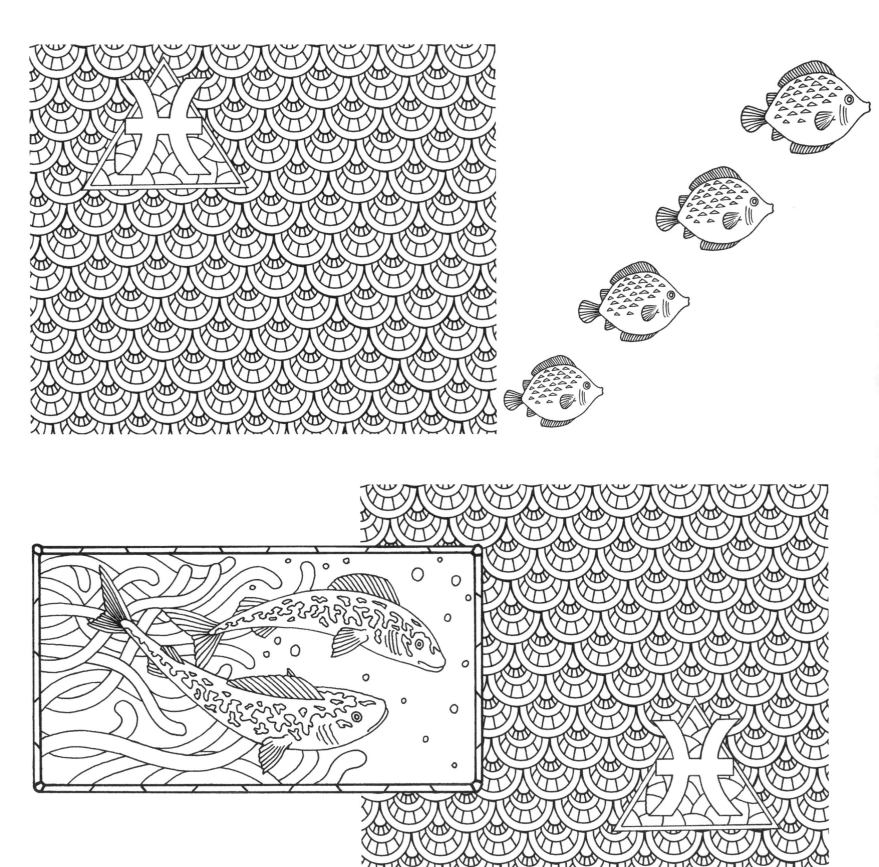

Black

Scorpio, Capricorn, Saturn and Pluto

From a teenage Goth to the chic 'little black dress' of Coco Chanel, this colour makes a dramatic entrance and holds the world in thrall. It is enigmatic, covert, surreptitious and secretive, just like everything in the naughty 'little black book'. Black is the underworld of Greek mythology; it is a colour to dread or one to embrace; it is the cloak-and-dagger thriller.

Jet black has its place but should be used carefully, as it indicates dominance and control in a destructive way. It can also, on a more positive note, suggest formality, tradition and psychological strength and power.

Invisible and hidden, black can cover up. Wearing the formidable colour gives an aura of menace or intimidation.

In some cultures, it is the shade worn by mourners at a funeral, so means bereavement, loss, grief and disappointment. Queen Victoria dressed in it for years after the loss of her Prince Consort, Albert, with jewellery made from jet, a black stone. Jet may be for mourning but it is also used as protection against psychic attacks or for resisting and repulsing negative and evil energies, so don't be afraid to use it.

Black is lascivious, sexual, obsessive and compelling. It is the bunny-boiler in a relationship; it is black, silky lingerie used to seduce and extract information; it is espionage and sexual conquest.

It is at its most sophisticated and glamorous when worn with gold, silver or precious stones. Black enhances and enriches brilliance. Wear it to look svelte and suave.

Black tie turns the ordinary occasion into something special. But black absorbs energy so it should be worn with care. All energies can be soaked up with this colour so wear white or silver to attract the light and reflect it outwards, illuminating your world. Let the sun shine in!

Black needs white to function positively. Yin cannot be free until plugged into yang (white).

If grey is the colour of shadows (see chapter on grey), then black hides. It withholds feelings and emotion, whilst white throws a revealing light on the clandestine places where black holds sway. A reputation can be 'blackened' or a person 'blackballed', ostracising someone from society.

Black can induce depression and doubt, so beams of white or silver are needed to shine a light on the dark and show the way to hope, optimism and happiness.

Black is the end of a cycle and white is the promise of a new chapter to come. In the ancients' calendar, when the sun disappears and leaves the world in darkness, to bring back the light, bonfires are lit to welcome back the sun.

Black can be used for good or ill, positive or negative; it is the colour of incredible power. Harness it and you have the key to transform and resurrect. Black can act as a catalyst and, used with a rich colour, it can spark regeneration and renewal.

Blue

Libra, Aquarius and Venus

In spiritual terms, blue is the colour of healing. Wearing royal or sky blue, as well as richer shades, can promote peacefulness and calm, and can help you on the path to restoration, recovery and tranquillity. It is said to be the world's favourite colour.

Blue brings balance when life is out-of-sorts and harmony is nowhere to be seen. It aids the relief of stress, tension and pressure. Living in a blue world makes life a little bit more bearable. Blue means a cool, calm and collected approach when everything's coming up less than rosy.

The term 'blue-sky thinking' describes a sense of liberation and a freedom of thought. If the Moon has been at the centre of musical lyrics ('Blue Moon'!) then so has the sky. 'Blue skies looking at me' is all about feeling good, feeling fine and believing that nothing's impossible.

Putting 'clear blue water' between one thing and another is a term for the obvious difference between ideas and ideologies of people from different persuasions, which highlights the individuality of the colour itself.

Dark blues can make you feel 'blue' just that bit too much and you might feel lost or lonely with little to look forward to. If this is the case, try adding a wee bit of a hot hue to your life.

This is also one helluva colour for communications. Laced with clever yellow, blue can mean the sky's the limit, it can convince and inspire verbally and, when it comes to speaking the wordsmith, has a mesmeric gaze to help bring out the best in people.

Having such a utopian and idealistic side, blue can inspire quixotic dreamers, and the expression 'sky-blue pink', which is a jocular name given to a non-existent colour, shows how ridiculous or wishful it can be.

Blue is a higher vibration on the spiritual colour spectrum, making it the perfect shade for those with strong beliefs or love of reclusive solitude, prayer and faith. Devotion and altruism on all levels is promised by blue. It promotes selflessness and wanting to help others, and is the colour for those wanting to pursue a healing vocation. Whatever the trouble, blue will always help a friend in need.

Blue is the colour of the seas but the shade depends upon the sky above it and reflecting on it, just as personal success in an ambition is reflected by the people a person has to work with or be guided by. The collective spirit is more important than the individual ego.

Shades of Blue...

Royal Blue/Ultramarine

This brilliant blue (made by grinding down the fabulous Lapis Lazuli stone) represents the most positive of qualities, but can also be conservative and low-key. It assumes control without ego getting in the way, for the greater good of others. Fidelity and loyalty comes with this shade of blue, as it's a fine, steadfast colour that promises fairness and justice; never wanting to belittle or undermine. A lack of or too much use of this powerful shade blocks feelings and leads to a cold or unemotional temperament.

Sky Blue

Freedom! Liberation! Liberal lashings of heavenly blue increases ingenuity with the hope to aspire to greater things. A glorious healing colour for when grief, despair or desperation strikes.

Azure

Said to be the colour of the sky on a clear summer's day. 'Azzurri' is a nickname bestowed on several national Italian sports teams, chosen for their flair and style. It represents hopes, dreams and aspirations in the most peerless of ways and a lack of this fabulous blue can lead to a personality that views the glass as half-empty.

Aquamarine

Whilst this pretty shade could be under green or blue, if you treat the stone to excessively high heat it will eventually change to a rich blue permanently. Just like the stone, aquamarine can transform, reducing anxiety and turning toxic feelings into kindness and even forgiveness.

Sapphire

This precious Sapphire blue promises to make an impact, Hollywood-style. As a gemstone, it inspires true love and affection. As a colour, it does the same. This blue reaches out the hand of friendship and allows you to find the perfect buddies.

Cobalt

Cobalt blue increases more matter-of-fact traits. It also brings out feelings of superiority, but creatively it produces works that are both useful and beautiful.

Prussian

This dark blue is ideal when duty and responsibility is required. Still waters run deep with this intense colour: hard to decipher it might be but Prussian blue provides an anchor in a wild sea. It is a popular corporate colour, impressing the image of dependability. A paucity of this colour allows the fickle or hypocritical to multiply, too much and austerity and a Victorian discipline takes root, but just enough gives integrity and a steady, guiding hand.

Cyan/Cornflower

Close to Lavender – remember the ditty 'Lavender's blue dilly-dilly'? Well, there you have it. A beautiful blue that warms up cool emotions. Use of it can bring relaxation where tension abounds. It is the original baby blue and, as they say, blue for a boy! Worn by a man, this can make them very attractive, as it highlights their handsome features. Could it be a magnet for love?

Brown

Taurus, Capricorn and Saturn

Brown is the good, rich earth beneath our feet It is the colour of terra firma and supports and nurtures in a strong, paternal way. Brown brings stability, strength and structure to everyday life.

If the Moon (Silver/White) is mother, Saturn (Brown) is father. Too much brown is authoritarian, officious, dictatorial and dogmatic, a hidebound Victorian; too little is weak, fragile, flimsy; just enough is protective, reliant and resilient. Accountability, responsibility and duty describes brown to a tee. It connects with the Mother and Father of the Moon/Saturn.

Having financial and material security is uppermost for this down-to-earth colour. Without tangible possessions or ownership of bricks-and-mortar, brown will find itself shifting in a world built on sand. Deep roots and foundations are what makes brown secure.

Overblown brown allows greed, cheapskates and penny-pinchers to proliferate. Brown prefers quality rather than quantity. Too little and there's a tendency to neglect personal appearance; scruffy and dirty. On the hunt for bargains, sometimes items are bought that aren't necessary or useful but it's worth it because they are cheap! Brown represents value-for-money.

Brown can be critical, scrutinising and carping, always reminding the world of a loss or upset, never forgetting a hurt or slight; hard-done-by and self-pitying. Positive brown is good to be around, familiar, antique and traditional with a dislike of surprises.

There is no such thing as a dreamer with brown around; it supports realism, pragmatism and organisation. 'Nothing is for nothing' is this earthy colour's motto, you get what you pay for and rewards are based on merit and darn hard work.

The joy of nature makes brown content and happy. It is organic, natural and wholesome. It is the colour of the agrarian, bucolic world and country living. Brown hates cities and the jarring reality that comes with a cheek-by-jowl existence. Space and time to reflect on life gives brown a boost, as it has a safe haven from the stresses of the outside world, a quiet place where problems can be contemplated and resolved. Far from the madding crowd and retiring into the shade away from the lime-light suits brown down to the ground.

A love of history and tradition, science and academia are attractive. Brown wants to learn and better themselves. Self-made men or women, successful in business: bring it on!

An old head on young shoulders, this colour promotes experience and wisdom that comes with maturity. There is a special quality for youth who are drawn to brown being older before their years. Brown is often viewed as boring and tedious but delve beneath the character of this colour and you have a solid, composed, upstanding quality required to survive in a modern world. It is the comforting and cosy base behind the more garish, vibrant hues.

Brown, green and blue are nature's colours and connect to our feelings and psyche, giving us something sane and normal to cling onto in a mad, mad, mad world.

Shades of Brown...

Sienna

Classy, arty and creative, Sienna brings richness and helps in the accumulation of wealth, making this shade a cut above the rest. Sienna suggests splendid business acumen.

Umber

A charcoal black, this colour can be melancholic but also prudent and practical. Seeing the negative and being too self-critical often excludes the fun factor, and Umber feels guilty or not worthy if they enjoy themselves. Reaching out for the approval of their peers can waste valuable time and is creatively limiting.

Ochre

Intellectually astute and able to come up with a clever twist to ordinary things, Ochre has a fine mind for business that can be applied to almost anything corporate.

Tan

A shade that relishes the simple life. An uncanny knack of being green-fingered or an animal-whisperer, Tan wants to go back to nature and stay there!

Ivory

In mythology, Pygmalion carved a beautiful woman from ivory and fell in love with her. This colour implies self-deception and an ability to live within dreams. This hue can enhance a love of beauty, as a positive, but this appreciation is ultimately lacking in emotion.

Beige/Fawn

Safety is the mainstay of these colours but too much can be dull and dreary. This enervating colour needs livening up by combining it with more vibrant shades or richer, darker browns.

Oatmeal

A colour of nature, the harvest and the good things of life. Oatmeal promises comfort and warmth without fuss and frills. Lovely with Cream!

Bronze/Copper

The lustre of Copper or Bronze brings the flat-earth of Brown to life. It daubs Autumn on walls and paintings, adding richness to ordinary hues, representing fulfilment and achievement. These shiny browns represent gifts gained on merit and diligence.

Gold

Leo, the Sun and Jupiter

Gold is the glittering prize the universe aspires to and wants to possess. But be warned that, in the words of Shakespeare, 'All that glisters is not gold'; just because it glitters, doesn't mean it's real.

To have gold is lucrative and the utmost in material security. It denotes prestige, recognition, wealth and pleasure. It encourages entrepreneurial talents and enterprising ideas. Gold shows prosperity, stability and success, whether it be on a crown, a ring or a stock market exchange board. If silver is feminine and lunar-linked then gold is masculine and solar-linked. Gold is the backdrop for precious stones to sparkle, dazzle and glitter at their very best. Gold is brilliance; being swathed in it projects prominence.

Gold is the winner; a gold medal means a triumph, first place in the competition. Turning base metals into gold has been the alchemist's mission for centuries, but to some it is a fool's gold. Whilst gold does suggest influence, affluence and power, it can also be hedonism, indulgence and decadence.

A surfeit of gold can be vain and arrogant, leading to an inflated ego and a narcissus complex. The tale of King Midas reveals this double-edged view of gold. The mythological king prayed that everything he touched turned to gold but he couldn't eat or drink, as the food once fingered metamorphosed into the precious metal, and he died of starvation.

Confidence, wisdom and generosity is as good as gold. Royalty, emperors and nobility wear gold to show their status. Add the imperial pomp of purple or the richness of red and it takes centre-stage, the award-winner. Gold is pure theatre, the star of stage and screen it fetes the fabulous and glamorous, and bedecks the prominent and influential. Negatively, it is nouveau-riche, vulgar and lacking in taste.

History is filled with cautionary tales of how too much gold can be dangerous. Overdo gold and a person is perceived as high-and-mighty, throwing their weight around, or bossy, unpleasant and a cut-above-the-rest.

Be bold in using gold. But maybe not too much.

Green

Taurus, Capricorn and Saturn

The most heartfelt colour is green. On the spiritual spectrum (chakra), green rules the heart (not red, as many would presume). There are seven centres physically, from the crown of the head to the root (base of the spine) and each centre is associated with a different colour. The heart chakra is the most central in the body.

Green aids the expression of feelings and emotions. This hue of renewal zaps a little bit of Spring into the Autumn of anyone's life. Green is growth, it enables a breakthrough of obstacles and puts a zing into the step of all to reduce fatigue or tiredness.

In feng shui, green is used for refuge, recovery and recuperation. It is ideal for the walls of a hospital, care home or clinic, as its soothing vibration aids rest and relaxation. Green grass, green leaves; green brings nature into a home or place of work.

Passive and positive green calms the savage breast and cools an aching heart. Loss or grief is placated by this hue to circulate compassion and charity to all.

The root of green is blue and yellow. Yellow is the colour of the mind and blue is the healing hue; together they increase crystal-clear clarity of mind, body and spirit.

Christmas is awash with greens and reds. A lack of green can make for a timid or unsure soul and red increases confidence and assertiveness. Green cools the anger and aggression of red, so together they are a perfect partnership, bringing cheer and merriment.

Green attracts people of a good heart and gentle soul. Wear green (especially emerald) to a celebration or event and you will attract someone towards you on a swift loving vibe. This colour is known to keep secrets and be strictly confidential; no fair-weather friend.

Flick through a wad of 'greenbacks' and you connect to this colour's ability to increase financial wealth, prosperity and abundance. Having money or cash in your pocket or purse should reflect some amount of safety and security for you and your world.

Beware, though. If you overdo the hue, then jealousy, envy, avarice and spite might take over the more kind and loving side of this heart-warming colour.

Shades of Green…

Spring Green

Ideal for making a fresh start. This green can induce a youthful spirit and joie de vivre, filling all with the joys of Spring. Not enough brings out immaturity and silliness that comes with callow youth or a lack of understanding of the decorum required in a grave situation.

Emerald

A personal favourite. A beautiful gemstone and a peerless colour, Emerald suggests abundance and prosperity, wealth and wellbeing, although this can also lead to greed or extravagance. You can always follow the yellow brick road to the Emerald City, as your personal Oz is within reach when bedecked in Emerald Green.

Jade

The colour of genuine love, virtue and longevity, plus sagacity and the ability to see through fakes and the flaws of others. A super shade that brings out the best in any situation: luck and serendipity leads to opportunity. Unconditional love melts the heart and attracts the truest friend.

Lime

This lively, vibrant green brightens the darkest days and eases sadness and depression. Like Spring Green, it is uplifting especially when people who are naturally zestful and hopeful are in your orbit.

Pine Green

Given its connotations of nobility, any use of Pine Green can suggest certain aspirations, whether in social or business circles. However, too much of a focus on this can imply a jealousy of others, and it is this envious streak that could lead to problems.

Olive/Khaki

You can offer the olive branch but khaki is also a colour of camouflage. Hiding your feelings and withholding information can create conflict at a later date. A measured amount shows you are a diplomat or pacifier; too much and you'll confuse others, and yourself, with your motivations.

Viridian

This exotic shade combines the unconditional love of green with the compassionate altruism of blue. Put the two together and you have Viridian, a shade which, when splashed all over, brings a sense of wellbeing and an ability to understand the needs of others.

Grey

Cancer, Capricorn, the Moon and Saturn

Dull, dull, dull! Though, is it? Well, not necessarily so. Grey is probably not everyone's cup of tea but it does a great job of being a conduit between stronger, vibrant, prime colours. Mind you, with *Fifty Shades of Grey* (I know it's the name of the guy) grey has had a make over and been reinvented as much more raunchy.

It is the diplomatic colour, a neutral hue, being a cocktail of black and white. It is not a million miles from silver but lacks the sparkle and dazzle of that metallic colour.

Grey has its own hidden depths, acting like a chameleon by taking on the vibe of other colours it is wed to. It is the colour of compromise: not enough and it becomes a ditherer and vacillator, too much and it's without focus or judgment. Just enough and it can hold things together, even emphasising the other colours. Grey is a great fixer.

Grey is distinguished, composed and sophisticated, with a simplicity that gives it a style and elegance all of its own. Grey is the dramatic beauty of black-and-white, of monochrome movies that become iconic, nostalgic and legendary. Some grumble that grey cannot be glamorous and begrudge this colour a kind of low-key beauty, but it can be glorious in its own way. The interplay between black and white has a drama that gives it continual appeal to the world of the arts and beyond.

Grey is resplendent in the hair of many older men and women, with connotations of class and a certain kind of mature beauty. A grey-haired man can be handsome and sexy, grey can still project a cool professionality and lend its user an air of authority.

Overwhelming grey can lead to an emotional cul-de-sac increasing doubt and even depression or despair, so, as with any colour, use in moderation and, particularly for grey, use to highlight the palette of the rest of the spectrum.

Shades of Grey...

Dove

The dove is the bird of peace and this colour instils calm. It soothes drama and hassle. Grey is seen as dreary but actually this shade is what you need in times of trouble. It gives you contact with your feelings and emotions through an attraction to the arts.

Battleship

Very conformist, mostly traditional and deadly serious. Its darkness represents discipline and dogma. You won't get round this colour through sweet talk. Unromantically inclined and relishing self-guilt, it is the colour of denial, formality and convention.

Stone

Verging on brown, Stone represents the meeting of two colours that are sturdy and stable. Stone allows for organisational ability and structure to flourish, and foundations to be laid. Form is given to the nebulous. A love of architecture and buildings bring out the best in this shade of grey: literally, a cornerstone colour.

Charcoal

Charcoal almost reaches the dramatic and intense power of black but is not quite as funereal. It doesn't have the deadness of pure black but can lift gloom, rendering self-help and self-sufficiency.

Taupe

A sleek, luxurious shade: a touch of mink. Bringing richness and old-fashioned style to stark and Spartan surroundings.

Indigo

Scorpio, Pisces, Neptune and Pluto

At the end of the rainbow there is a crock of gold. But is the gold material wealth or spiritual enrichment? The answer is spiritual enrichment, for this is the colour of intuition, perception and psychic powers. Spiritual wisdom and knowledge abounds.

Indigo triggers the far-seeing third eye and connects the sixth sense with the other five. Drape this colour in a natural fabric, like satin or silk, around you to transcend the ordinary into the extraordinary.

The power of indigo runs through disciplines such as yoga, meditation and contemplation, and encourages astral travel. It brings an explosion of inner peace, drenching the spirit in a divine indescribable bliss. It is the colour of the higher mind and higher consciousness.

Indigo even increases faith in religion and belief. It is a colour of mourning in the Christian faith, and of ritual and tradition. The altar is covered with a purple cloth on Good Friday as a symbol of dignity, piety, devotion and sincerity.

Indigo is an amalgam of the deepest of blues, the richness of purple or violet and is emboldened by shades of red, making it incredibly powerful and interesting. Even the name is exotic, coming from the plant used for dyeing.

Anyone drawn to this enigmatic, mysterious colour craves status and has the tantalising ability to reach their goal by seduction and sexuality. Wear indigo to give an unconventional aura that bewitches and excites. Telepathic communication is increased via this colour.

An excess of indigo gives delusions of grandeur, creates a diva or divo and increases intolerance and prejudice. Too much causes resentment when others appear to have more than you or, worse, what you want. It makes for an obsessive or fanatic, someone who has a tendency to become addicted to narcotics to increase escapism. The thin dividing line between genius and madness is walked if this colour gets out of control, so organisation is a must; this shade can allow chaos to abound.

An elegant sufficiency of this shade makes for a highly evolved soul reaching for spiritual perfection. Unconditional in their love for others, including animals, these souls are heavenly in wanting to help and rescue those in need. Aid workers, humanitarians and those fighting for the rights of the poor or underprivileged are attracted to indigo.

Indigo is negative for those of a nervous disposition or depressive personality. It can worsen the mood, as the so-called 'Mood Indigo' can create inner turmoil and distress.

An intense indigo energy stimulates the right side of our brains, the section used for creative activity. It sparks super-intelligence and helps you to get your head around puzzles and predicaments.

Magenta/Cerise

Aries, Libra, Scorpio, Mars and Venus

These two luxurious, opulent colours reflect one another like a photographic negative. Magenta combines red and violet, and cerise (coming from the French for cherry) is a rich pink.

Together they project spiritual harmony, reaching out with love and kindness. These colours promise a sumptuous tenderness and sensational softness, and their rich hues warm harsh and drab environments.

Magenta or cerise create equilibrium where there is crisis due to sadness, disappointment or upset. These colours help to avoid vacillation and indecision when trying to overcome life's setbacks and traumas. Ideal for evading procrastination and prevarication.

There is as much passion as love in these hot hues, a saucy vibe if you will. With red at their heart, they can be very lusty and lascivious if over-used, but at the same time have hints of cooling blues, violets and whites to melt the damaging effects away. Magenta and cerise give you the best of all possible worlds.

The spiritual potential of these colours are ideal for regenerating your life, and show a disposal of the old and welcoming in of the new. If you are tied to a challenging emotional or psychological situation then these colours show you breaking free, creating a fresh chapter and making a fresh start.

You don't get better than magenta or cerise in repairing a broken affair, as they send healing, love, forgiveness and understanding. Reconciliation is more than possible by sending a letter or card enriched with one or other of these positive shades. These colours promote happiness and the hopeful feeling that something better is just around the corner.

These deluxe colours spur ambition, as they have a knack of transforming dreams to reality. There is attraction to the unconventional, random and unusual, a path to success. The risqué, avant-garde energy within both these colours can be used to turn heads and influence people, turning on the tap of ingenuity for creative projects and artistic writing, painting and music.

Opposites attract so 'odd couple' relationships are possible. A mismatch on the outside can become a perfect match in reality. Even if a relationship appears bizarre or odd actually there is a harmony. There is a magnetism and charisma that crackles, zips and sizzles along with such a delectable desire giving an irresistible appeal.

A wee word of warning: because of the violet within it, magenta can smother a room and lead a naturally negative person into a downward-spiral. It should be used as a hint or a tint rather than the all-out va-va-voom colour. Be sparing with cerise around lazy types, as it can increase the lackadaisical to become too relaxed.

Orange

Leo, Sagittarius and the Sun

Think of the tango, a lustrous dance filled with passion and heat. The use of orange can inject a whole load of both of these into your soul and into your life.

It is the colour of elevation and of renewal, giving a mental and physical boost. Were it to be represented in music, its theme tune would be 'Always Look On the Bright Side of Life'.

Orange is formed from the combination of red and yellow so you can get a fix of both colours; drive and vitality from red, and intellectual and cerebral power from yellow. Put a little orange in your life and you will feel mentally and physically inspired.

There is something theatrical about this colour. There's no business like showbusiness if the stage is alive with flamenco orange. If you want to take a lead or starring role in your life then you win Oscars with this!

Orange inspires social communication and its lively hue will imbue any party with fun and laughter. It opens up the door to getting on with everyone.

Shades of Orange…

Apricot/Peach

If orange can often encourage people to be over-the-top then this pastel shade encourages manners, courtesy and genteel conversation. It is said that when used too much it can lead to infidelity.

Topaz

Gives the positive power of deep thinking and endows an inquiring mind. It imbues wanderlust with a love of travel and enjoyment of faraway places.

Amber

The feel-good factor comes with amber. However, if it is overdone then it can lead to acting superior to others. In mythology, it is said to relieve grief, sadness and melancholy.

Sienna

This rich orange-brown can give a touch of class. It enriches even the most ordinary with understated nobility, but use it sparingly or it can give the impression of someone who is materialistic and self-obsessed.

Pink

Libra, Taurus and Venus

Hands up if you thought Red was the colour of love? Well, it is the colour of passion and desire but Pink is the colour of abiding love; giving yourself to someone but wanting it reciprocated. Overdo the pink and suggest a sense of unrequited love, so if using it in your life, such as in decorating your room (especially the bedroom), make sure that it echoes your vision of love.

Pink is the colour of union, commitment and marriage. It brings two people together in loving partnership. Relationships prosper under pink.

There is a gentility and compassion that comes with pink. For women, it projects elegance and femininity, and, given these factors, with men it can reveal a softer side, an ease with their sexuality. The changing perceptions of gender through the ages may alter the meaning of pink, but this is always a colour that gives love to all.

Pink comes from a combination of red and white, with the white calming the lustiness of the red and creating a romantic shade. It shrugs off loneliness and attracts situations or people who love each other for who they are; an honesty that means there's no need to pretend.

Pink is an attractive colour to those going through a bad time; it reassures and gives hope even at the most difficult or challenging periods in your life. Here's a fact: criminals imprisoned for GBH, violence or worse have been calmed down by being in a pink room for a period of time.

Although pink is about caring and compassion, too much of it can reveal a needy soul. You know the maxim about radiators? Some are an emotional drain while others give out heat through love. Going crazy with pink can expose a craving for acceptance or approval, but just enough shows a sharing, caring person.

Colouring your world with too much pink might scream immaturity, silliness and childish behaviour; the girly giggles or queenie behaviour that can drive a person crazy.

This sweet colour produces precisely that: a sweet nature. Sufficient amounts can promote courtesy, diplomacy and sincerity. Not enough can reveal something more selfish. Whether it be ingratitude and a lack of grace or cowardice and greed, never happy with what they've got, always searching or looking for more or the unattainable, a lack of pink is a lack of love.

For shades, please see page 105.

Shades of Pink…

Soft Pink

A lack of commitment and strength. Using this pink means you are liable to give up on a project or affair before it's even begun. It's fine to encourage a first flush of love, but will it last?

Rose

A powerful pink used to portray the richest love, it is ideal to propagate a relationship. Roses sent in this colour proffer empathy and compassion, as well as the softest, warmest, most tender and heartfelt emotions.

Coral

Said in mythology to encourage potency in love and to increase intimacy. But be warned: this hue is great for a one-night-stand but nothing more enduring. It is flirtatious and can lead to mixed messages.

Hyacinth

Unusual and avant-garde. The use of this floral pink suggests you're an independent individual who wants to do their own thing.

Fuchsia

Fabulously exciting. This colour attracts a mature love and indicates a person who knows themselves and is even confident in sex. Love is lovelier the second time around for this shade.

Shocking Pink

Shockingly hot, this is the hue used by Gay Pride and gay rights. It is passionate, outrageous, seductive and sensual. It inspires passionate, playful and sensual love. Spread a little happiness by giving prominence to this explosive pink.

Purple and Violet

Jupiter, Sagittarius and Pisces

There is a subtle but definite difference between purple and violet. Violet appears in the visible light spectrum, or rainbow, whereas purple is a simple mix of red and blue. Violet has the highest vibration in the rainbow and gives it a spiritual edge on all other colours.

Purple (personally, my favourite colour) is the highest form of consciousness in the chakra. It is the most spiritual of all colours, sparking the imagination and psychic abilities.

Purple represents the highest ideals of the individual and promises insight into our unconscious mind, so if this mystical colour dominates your dream then look for the deeper current of meaning running through it.

Violet, though not as intense as purple, has a similar essence. Both contain the raw energy of red stirred with the gentle spirituality of blue; each a body-and-soul cock-tail of colour merging physical and spiritual energies.

Sages, psychics and philosophers are drawn to purple and violet. Their alchemy leads to transformation of the old and an ability to detach from anything beyond its prime. Too much gives a wild imagination (and can lead to addiction to drugs or alcohol to escape the real world). Too little and the spiritual soul remains earthbound. Just enough brings the pursuit of enlightenment and the chance to explore the hidden avenues of life whilst remaining grounded.

Music, art and dance feed the purple/violet soul. A love of grace, elegance and joy is found in echelons of beauty from opera to ballet. This colour inspires the poet and writer.

There is a magical vibration emanating when worn or surrounded by it. Never part of the in-crowd, these colours encourage the unworldly and ethereal. Ultra-violet adds to the allure of an ordinary place, as its invisibility to the eye is suggestive of a fantasy world under the visible surface.

Violets or purples are also the most sensitive in the world of colour. They seek peace and quiet, hating noise on any level. An unconditional soul searching for perfection, they feel out of place or lost avoiding loud crowds or locations that make them uncomfortable. Health can be affected by the polluted side of the modern world, but, while it may be preferable to live in a bubble and not deal with the ugliness of life, it is not ideal.

The luxury and richness of purple and, to a lesser extent, violet is perhaps why it is known to be a noble colour, associated with the royal lives of emperors and kings. A touch of purple gives the impression of success and self-assurance that fits with a higher station. However, its deep spirituality is another reason why this colour befits a ruler: they are those without a thought for themselves. They are saintly without being a martyr.

Like indigo, purple and violet should be used in small doses by people prone to melancholy, as it can increase depression. These colours are potent, so be mindful and beware of overdoing it.

For shades, please see page 107.

Shades of Purple and Violet…

Lavender

Said to be the colour of fairy-land, this colour is attractive to people who are sensitive and who have a love of beauty.

Lilac

A gentle lilac leads to love but can increase fickleness. Romantic and gay, this colour attracts souls who want a wonderland filled with beauty.

Mauve

Mauve isn't as royal as purple or as supernatural as violet. It strikes a more mundane tone, appealing to the everyday woman or man.

Amethyst

The richness of amethyst when worn as a stone or used on walls and fabrics militates against drabness. It helps those who fall prey to mundane worries and fears or who are prone to domination by more controlling individuals. In ancient times, it was dropped into liquids to see if they were poisoned and was said to work against drunkenness.

Plum/Aubergine

Plum is a reddish purple. This is a love-or-hate purple. It promotes the sceptical or cynical if overused, but just enough can enhance pride, raising familial noblesse oblige.

Deep Purple

A powerful, spiritual colour. Surrounding yourself with this colour will help open your third eye, but be warned, as it can make for susceptibility to false prophets or a distorted view of living. Too much shows self-esteem but to the point of vanity. Tone it down and it can enliven an aura with love for others rather than yourself.

Red

The Colour of Aries, Scorpio and Mars

This superhero colour is go, go, go if you want to excite positive, proactive and progressive action. Red stimulates passion and desire; it'll get you all fired-up. It's the trigger to setting off the libido and imbues stamina and sex appeal if you are focussing on something or someone you want. Think flame-hot lippie!

If pink is love then red is sex. Too much red and it becomes lust. Feeling drained or down? Red will increase your metabolism and your get-up-and-go.

It is the colour of the adventurer and pioneer. If you are a go-getter getting nowhere then red will reveal a deep need to increase your adrenaline, stamina and the need to be a risk-taker. The blood is up! Yes, that's red too. Increased red corpuscles in the veins can help athletic prowess and personal strength. Get down to the gym!

If you are diffident, unsure or lacking in confidence a good dose of red gives you the nerve and verve to believe in yourself.

Red represents competitive spirit but overdo it and it can release an argumentative or aggressive personality. Just enough and you can achieve what you want to win, too much and you destroy those things you wish to cherish. A need for cooling colours will moderate incandescent anger: try blues and greens.

With Feng Shui and astrological design, red can increase anger, impatience and recklessness, so it should be used sparingly. Too little makes for timidity and shyness that can irritate or oppress others. Just enough will trigger positive vibes and help initiate new, fresh and exciting projects.

Shades of Red...

Maroon

Heightens thoughtful concentration. You become aware that all actions have consequences.

Burgundy/Wine

This rich colour defines nobility and royalty. It imbues judgement and wisdom that comes through experience and maturity. Using it increases honour and integrity.

Crimson

Lust is turned to sensuality. Crimson means a desire for passion, from the arts to love-making. It's all about the senses.

Scarlet

You can't help but think of *Gone with the Wind* and Scarlett O'Hara. Scarlet gives a vivacious outlook and a live-for-moment attitude.

Vermilion

This rich hue channels a love of the arts and increases creative flow. It gives attraction to things artistically historic and beautiful, especially when used with gold.

Ruby

Ruby adds lustre and richness, even to dazzling red. It increases passion and promises everlasting love. Desire for something or someone makes this lush shade ideal for success in affairs of the heart. It lights the flame of wisdom. Wherever this intense red is used, it gives heat and power.

Silver

Cancer, Aquarius, the Moon and Uranus

The silvery Moon and the tides have been connected since time immemorial. The Moon controls the seas and oceans with the ebb and flow of the tides and it is this same fluidity that makes silver emotional, hypersensitive, gentle, sympathetic, nostalgic and compassionate.

Like white, silver purifies, and, like the moon, it reflects the ambience and energy of the atmosphere around it. Silver illuminates dark places and reveals the hidden and covert nooks, crannies and crevices. It helps to relieve heavy psychological, cerebral and emotional stress, giving a carapace of protection.

The silver vibration, psychically, is said to reach to the highest level in clairvoyance and mediumship. It is even higher than purple or violet on the spiritual continuum, as silver reaches out beyond the earthbound into the supernatural. Consciousness and psychic powers are two different things.

If gold is masculine then silver is feminine. This metallic colour links with Minerva/Athena, the goddess of wisdom. But she is also the goddess of war. Silver is unfeeling and mentally astute, able to rationalise and manifest answers to questions in an intuitive way. Feminine intuition hits new heights with silver, giving it stunning luminosity.

Silver is related to grey more than white. It gives a regal, respectable, distinguished, dignified air to every corner of the world it inhabits. It grants added lustre and beauty in jewellery, and it is this natural allure that makes it preferable for many technological investigations. Silver is spectacular!

Shimmering silver is connected with maturity; silver hair can be a sign of beauty and wisdom that comes with age. Silver is a shining light revealing dishonesty, injustice and unfairness.

Reflecting varying qualities can also make silver deceptive, two-faced and surreal. You can make a silver purse out of a sow's ear but it will always be a sow's ear. It is the bling on a singer's and dancer's costume; even with crystal rather than precious stones silver will still make it look real, authentic and genuine. It will look good until you get up close and personal and realise it's fake!

Silver works with all colours as it reflects the glory of the rainbow to the world around it, but in order to radiate love and good feelings, it needs to be coupled with warm colours. Mystique and fantasy, however, come naturally to those that use a lot of silver, so coupling it with a number of colours (including grey, black, blue and purple) will bring out these qualities.

Turquoise

Capricorn, Aquarius, Mercury, Venus and Uranus

Turquoise is a higher-minded colour on the spiritual spectrum and is said to be extremely protective. The turquoise stone is at the centre of the Eye of Fatima, known as the evil eye, and can help repulse intrusion and attack from dark, evil forces. In ancient cultures and civilisations, this colour was placed in burial grounds to attract guardian goodly spirits, like gargoyles on a church. As a healing stone and a healing colour, it will relax a troubled mind or spirit, so use it when under pressure to lessen tension.

Turquoise lightens the load of a heavy day. It increases eloquent and articulate communication between people. Bonding with friends honestly and openly is on the turquoise vibration.

As a colour, it controls excess of feelings and negates emotional neediness. Although not sympathetic (like green or aquamarine), it maintains a balance after loss or trauma. The use of turquoise helps heal a wounded heart from bereavement, grief or sadness, and can even ease loneliness by turning quiet and solitude into calmness and tranquillity.

This colour helps seek and find a quiet space to retire away and lick emotional or psychological wounds. Once recovered, it gives inner strength and assists second chances. The link with the sign Aquarius and planets Mercury and Uranus makes it an ideal stone for doing more than one thing at once; hot-desking and multi-tasking. The boredom threshold of this colour is low, so it aches to try new things and be creatively inventive. There are only a few colours linked to karma (the spiritual law of cause-and-effect) and turquoise is one of them. It is the old soul who has been round the reincarnational block and has just one colour to go: purple. A most spiritual colour, like blue, it is used for healing and increasing spiritual awareness.

Too much of this rich colour can suggest selfishness and self-obsession. Just enough promotes unconditional humanitarian love for their fellow man or woman. A dearth of turquoise reveals a lack of spiritual knowledge, making feeble excuses to avoid involvement in others' problems; a fence-sitter! Turquoise helps dismiss worries and ease the pain of paranoia or neuroses through kindness and wise advice that spouts from a spiritual fount.

Shades of Turquoise…

Aqua

Can there ever be a colour more refreshing and tingling than this? It calms and relaxes. It inspires a splash of brilliance. Aqua rejuvenates!

Teal

Classy and assured, this colour strengthens unbalanced emotions. It makes for self-assurance and a trusted, honourable reputation.

Peacock

Exotic, luxurious, tantalising and enticing, this colour must be used sparingly. A little goes a long way and too much can lead to self-centredness and narcissism. Over-the-top peacock is blind to what's going on around but be brave and use it well to stop being overlooked and stuck in a rut. The right amount will grant the courage to dump boredom and seek excitement.

White

Cancer, Virgo and the Moon

Innocent, new, clean, chaste, pristine… all describe white. White is the vestal virgin, the bride sweeping down the aisle in white silk. Whether Snow White in the fairy tale or the whitest of knights, Sir Galahad, in shining armour riding to rescue some poor soul in distress, there is always one consistency with white: purity.

White is a fresh start and new beginnings. It is the clean sheet of white, spotless paper waiting for other colours to create something beautiful. Neutral white is an equal balance, a union and harmony, of all colours in the spectrum. Spiritually, it is the gleaming, brilliant white light that leads to a greater world of psychic understanding and esoteric enlightenment.

If white is cleanliness and you apply those character -istics to a room, then it can reflect a state of mind. Too much is bare, almost obsessively so. Too little shows a cluttered, messy, untidy life where confusion reigns and where powerful colours predominate, perverting the purity of this colour.

White is cold, lacking and unemotional. White requires richness from other hues to bring out its clear, reflective qualities and to illuminate the rest of the rainbow. White itself has no heart, no feeling. It fails to inspire by itself, but can be used powerfully with strong colours.

White puts nerves on edge and can stop people feeling comfortable. Its sense of emptiness can increase feelings of isolation and loneliness, but when used with greens and blues, white can entice with the promise of calm and sympathy.

White can represent many things; peace, as the release of white doves symbolic of worldwide peace; purification, as it's all that's left in the wake of the toxic and polluting spectrum; and even new life, as it is used in the western world for weddings and in other countries to show death. It opens the door to a new life chapter, sweeping clear rubbish and mess from the past. It cleans and refreshes. White is the blank page on which you can start colouring in.

Yellow

Gemini, Virgo and Mercury

Yellow is the colour of the mind and intellect. This colour, which is representative of the planet Mercury, is linked to the left (or logical) side of the brain; dealing with mental agility, intellectual faculties and the way we think and express ourselves.

The brightness of yellow, like sunshine, reigns supreme for easing depression and disappointment. Lashings of yellow can lavish happiness, hope and optimism on a sad mind. A life without yellow is a dark life, spoilt by disappointment and disillusion. It can heighten anxiety and pedantry.

The brain responds to this daylight colour positively with an increased amount of curiosity and inquisitiveness. Such an active, open mind can help with decision-making, enabling to rationally weigh up advantages and disadvantages needed to make the right choice.

However, this can also cause problems. Too much yellow can lead to anxiety through over-thinking a delicate or obvious situation, making a drama out of a crisis; a mountain out of a molehill. Too little yellow can indicate a dreamer, rather than someone who is inventive and practical. Just enough promotes cerebral brilliance within us all. To feed the mind, try a puzzle. A Rubik's cube challenge or a crossword is the food for thought that yellow loves.

While too much red or pink rules the heart, yellow rules the head, so a mixture will provide a good balance between head and heart.

Shades of Yellow...

Sunflower

Enables your wits to be honed, as (cerebrally) it makes for a bright-eyed and bushy-tailed spirit.

Lemon

Gives the positive power of deep thinking and endows an inquiring mind. It imbues wanderlust with a love of travel and enjoyment of faraway places.

Citrine

In Crystology, citrine is used to increase money and wealth but, most importantly, to find a solution to financial problems. It can also be very superficial, promoting social butterflies who flit here and there.

Cream

Brings warmth and a cosy, settled feeling. There is a sentimental or nostalgic link. Lots of cream can mean living in the past but just enough underpins a mental balance achieving softness. Not enough can lead to not venturing beyond the familiar.

Daffodil

Brightens the soul with an optimistic outlook and constructive criticism. Not enough of this type of yellow may result in constant carping and a lack of satisfaction. The condition SAD (Seasonal Affective Disorder) can lead to melancholy and even depression, but adding a vase of daffodils to any room should help avoid this!

Vanilla

Likes to play safe. Is content with the familiar and the usual. Not a risk-taker but happy with the status-quo.